ALL MADRID

6th Edition, March 1984

I.S.B.N.

Spanish	84-378-0420-5
French	84-378-0422-1
English	84-378-0424-8
Italian	84-378-0465-5

Dep. Legal B. 9031-1984

 **escudo de oro, s.a.** Palaudarias, 26 - Barcelona, 4 - Spain

Impreso en España - Printed in Spain
F.I.S.A. Palaudarias, 26 - Barcelona-4

A view of the Plaza Mayor as it was at the time of the proclamation of Fernando VII as king, from an engraving of the period.

An attractive night time view of the Segovia bridge with boats moving on the waters of the Manzanares almost giving it the look of a real sea port.

A partial view of Madrid from the Segovia bridge.

A fine close-up of the popular Puerta del Sol. ▷

MADRID, CAPITAL OF SPAIN

The name Madrid apparently comes from the Arab word *Magerit,* although according to Menéndez Pidal, it could also be derived from the word *Mageterito,* of Celtic origin. Situated in the geographical centre of the Iberian peninsula at a height of 650 metres above sea level, Madrid is built right in the middle of the Castilian plateau on hills at whose feet flows the river Manzanares.

Judging by finds from the paleolithic and neolithic periods and the Bronze Age in the valley of the Manzanares, near to what is now Madrid, the region was already inhabited in prehistoric times. But the real history of Madrid began with the Arabs when, in the year 852, Mohammed I captured the Visigothic settlement which then occupied the area between the calle Mayor and the calle Bailén. In 1083, Alfonso VI during whose reign the patron saint of Madrid, St. Isidro was born, took the town for the Christians. Almost two

centuries later, in 1262, Alfonso X, the Wise, gave Madrid its Royal Rights.

Madrid's historical rank began to be established around 1392 when the parliament convened by Fernando IV met there, and when Enrique III was proclaimed king. Ferdinand and Isabella went to Madrid for the first time in 1477 and the modernization and extension of the city is due to them.

The consecration of Madrid as the capital of Spain was carried out by Philip II in 1561, and this was a definite step forward historically, although in the time of Philip III, the court was for several years in Valladolid. The House of Austria made Madrid a capital with a distinctive architectural style. Later on, Philip V and Charles III made it into a modern city with an extraordinary wealth of monuments. Madrid kept on growing throughout the XIX and XX centuries until it became, after 1939, one of the most densely populated and dynamic capitals in Europe, with broad avenues, residential areas and ultra modern buildings.

A monument to the Bear and the Strawberry Tree — the symbols of the city — standing in the middle of the Puerta del Sol.

The centre of Spain; all the streets of Madrid and the motorways of Spain radiate from this point in the Puerta del Sol.

A night time view of the Puerta del Sol.

THE PUERTA DEL SOL

This is perhaps the most popular square in Spain. It is thus called because the sun shone in through one of the postern gates in the walls which stood there in the XVI century, in the part now occupied by the square; this wall was apparently demolished in the second half of the XVI century. The Puerta del Sol, until 1978 was considered the geographical centre of Madrid. Now, according to the official atlas of the civic authorities of Madrid, the centre of the capital of Spain is in the gardens of the Prado Museum, opposite the staircase leading to the church of San Jerónimo el Real, this being due to the great expansion of the area of Madrid during the last few years. But the Puerta del Sol has not lost any of its popularity because of this. It is a place that is always visited by everyone who comes to Madrid for the first time and also where, every New Year's Eve, a vast crowd gathers to eat the traditional twelve grapes, to the rhythm of the twelve strokes of midnight by the clock on the former Ministry of Home Affairs building.

The front of the Monastery of the Descalzas Reales.

An impressive close-up of
the Monastery of San
Jerónimo el Real taken at
night.

An evocative spot in the
old part of Madrid.

A night time view of the
Town Hall.

A nocturnal shot of the historical Plaza Mayor.

The lovely Casa de Panadería in the Plaza Mayor. ▷

THE PLAZA MAYOR

This is one of the loveliest and architecturally most balanced squares in Europe. Its majestic, original style is an outstanding example of the prevalent characteristics of the period of the House of Austria in Spain. The Plaza Mayor was built on the orders of Philip III and work on it was begun in 1617, under the direction of Juan Gómez de Mora, being completed in 1619.

Rectangular in structure, the square is 200 metres long by 100 metres wide and is surrounded by enormous porticoes, under which are numerous restaurants, bars and shops. The Plaza Mayor has ten archways with as many gates leading to the inner precinct: Ciudad Rodrigo, Cuchilleros, Toledo, Botoneras, Gerona, Zaragoza, la Sal, Philip III, el Triunfo, and Siete de Julio. In the centre of the square stands a magnificent equestrian statue of Philip III sculpted by Pedro Tacca and cast by Juan de Bolonia.

During the period of the House of Austria, the Plaza Mayor was made up of 136 houses, and from their balconies the most varied selection of festivities and spectacles could be seen — from autos da fe, to bull-fights, and the proclamation of the coming of age of the kings of Spain from Philip IV to Isabel II.

An outstanding feature of the magnificent architectural personality of the Plaza Mayor is the Real Casa de Panadería where part of the city archives are kept.

A night time close-up of the evocative Arco de Cuchilleros.

Three animated scenes from the world of the taverns.

THE CUISINE OF MADRID

Madrid is one of the cities in Europe which offers some of the best and most varied of foods. There are many restaurants and inns where you can eat any of the typical dishes of the repertoire of Spanish regional cooking, from the delightful cod *al pil-pil* or the unforgettable *cocochas* from the Basque country, to the popular Valencian *paella,* the succulent pork with turnip tops, and the exquisite shell fish from Galicia, the bean stew from Asturias, sausages from Catalonia and the magnificent roast sucking pig and lamb Castilian style. There are also the genuine dishes of Madrid such as, *el cocido* (stew) and tripe in a piquant sauce. On the other hand, it is equally possible to enjoy the most refined specialities of international gastronomy, — Italian *pizzas* and *osobucco*, German sauerkraut, Chinese dishes, Russian caviar and *churrasco* (roast meat) from Argentina.

Worthy of special mention are the *tascas* of Madrid (popular bars) where, together with a glass of wine or a glass of beer you can eat the most varied and appetizing *tapas* (small savoury dishes).

The typical Madrid stew (el cocido), *an appetizing dish.*

Tripe, Madrid style, another typical dish.

Chocolate *with* churros, *the Madrid breakfast par excellence.*

The San Isidro Meadow, *a festivity made immortal by Goya.*

THE SAN ISIDRO MEADOW

In former times a popular feast was celebrated in honour of the patron saint of Madrid in the meadow surrounding the Hermitage of San Isidro. Nowadays, in the middle of May, the Madrid feast of San Isidro is still celebrated, as well as that of San Antonio de la Florida beside the Manzanares in June, the feast of Las Vistillas and La Paloma in San Francisco in August, and the feast of La Almudena in the middle of the month of September. Madrid's most important feast days are those celebrated in honour of San Isidro, which last a fortnight and, during this time there are big bull-fights every day and different celebrations, in the various districts.

MADRID BY NIGHT

The capital of Spain offers a considerable repertoire of entertainment at night. There are an infinite number of night clubs, discothèques, night time shows with dancers, jazz rooms, pop music and intellectual cafés. But perhaps the most attractive feature of night life in Madrid, especially for foreigners, is the *tablaos,* where the most outstanding artists in the world of Flamenco dancing perform. All those fond of what is known as *cante chico* —light and jovial—, and *cande jondo* —more profound and charged with emotion—, have in Madrid, a wide choice of places where they can hear Flamenco music and see the best of Flamenco dancers.

Two aspects of the dynamic night life of the Gran Vía, an Andalusian dance group and one of the streets filled with bars to be found near the Plaza Mayor.

THE CENTRE OF MADRID

Between the Plaza del Callao and the Plaza de la Cibeles, the Puerta del Sol and the Plaza de España, the Gran Vía and the streets of Alcalá, Montera and Fuencarral, stretches an urban area of great commercial vitality, inundated at all hours by masses of people. The traffic here is also very dense. This is a part of Madrid which was built for the most part at the beginning of this century and which acquired its airs of a great city during the last forty years. The junction of the Gran Vía and the calle de Alcalá is a vital link in

The junction of the calle de Alcalá and the Gran Vía.

The façade of the church of Las Calatravas, dating from the XVII century.

A view of the calle de Alcalá, the Puerta de Alcalá and the Retiro Park.

this area. The Gran Vía starts in the calle de Alcalá and ends in the Plaza de España. It is a busy street full of vitality with both pavements always bursting with people, and the road filled with cars. On both sides of the Gran Vía are several luxury hotels, magnificent shops, jewellers, cinemas, book shops and night clubs. Almost at the beginning of the Gran Vía is the baroque church of San José and a little further on, on the same side of the road, is the bar of Perico Chicote, famous in the 1940s, where there still exists a curious Drinks Museum.

Another important and very popular street in this part of the city is the calle de Alcalá which begins in the Puerta del Sol and reaches the bull-ring of Las Ventas. This is an elegant, but at the same time popular street, always busy, especially in the part where it begins, up to the Puerta de Alcalá; it is one of the most characteristic streets in Madrid and along its considerable length are monuments such as the statue of Cibeles and the Puerta de Alcalá and the entrance to the Retiro Park. This street is flanked by several important buildings, among them the Banco de España, the Buenavista Palace, the Communications Palace and the Ministry of Finance, also the Museum of the Royal Academy of Fine Arts of San Fernando where one of Goya's most famous paintings entitled *The Burial of the Sardine* can be seen. The streets of Montera and Fuencarral add to the dynamic character of the area as does the motly and bustling Plaza del Caudillo.

A splendid night time view of the calle de Alcalá with the Cibeles fountain in the foreground.

A magnificent close-up of the Cibeles fountain, one of Madrid's most popular monuments.

Cibeles, with the Palace of Communications in the background.

THE PLAZA DE LA CIBELES

This is one of the most popular squares in Madrid and indeed in the whole of Spain. The statue and fountain were built in the time of Charles III. The popular monument, completed in 1792 was originally sited at the beginning of the Paseo de Recoletos, but was brought to its present location a century later.

The statue of the goddess was made according to a design by Ventura Rodríguez. The figure of Cibeles was sculpted in Montesclaros marble by the court sculptor Francisco Gutiérrez, while the lions are the work of Roberto Michel.

The fountain, with its elegant jets of illuminated water, makes a lovely sight at night.

A close-up of the Apollo fountain.

The Cibeles fountain and a night time view of the Palace of Communications.

An impressive close-up of the Puerta de Alcalá.

THE PUERTA DE ALCALA

This undoutbtedly is one of the loveliest and most architecturally distinctive monuments in the capital. Situated in the calle de Alcalá, close by Cibeles and beside the Retiro Park, the Puerta de Alcalá was constructed in 1778 with a triumphal archway built in honour of Charles III for his entry into the city as king of Spain.

The monument is solid and compact made from granite and limestone from Colmenar. Originally projected by Ventura Rodríguez, it was Francisco Sabatini who was finally commissioned to design it. The Puerta de Alcalá is a construction with five entrances, the three in the centre having half pointed arches and the two lateral ones being straight. Francisco Gutiérrez and Roberto Michel, the authors of the monument to Cibeles were also those responsible for the sculpted decoration on the Puerta de Alcalá. The harmonious structure of the monument is held up by ten columns in ionic style, with a well balanced corniced attic on the top. Among the decoration on the monument is a large coat of arms held aloft by Fame and Genius and several lions' heads. The Puerta de Alcalá which is situated in the Plaza de la Independencia with the streets of Serrano and Alfonso XII leading off it, is surrounded by attractive, well looked after flower beds. This popular monument is one of the most characteristic and best known scenes in Madrid.

The Puerta de Alcalá, under whose arches passes the popular street of the same name.

Statue to the famous bull-fighter Antonio Bienvenida.

BULLS

Besides the Monumental de las Ventas bull-ring which is the high cathedral of bull-fighting in Spain, Madrid has an important bull-fighting establishment in Vista Alegre in Carabanchel Bajo. To be successful in either of these two arenas, especially during the San Isidro festivities, is always the making of a bull-fighter on his road to fame.

In Las Ventas there is an interesting bull-fighting Museum.

A fine view of the Monumental de las Ventas bull-ring.

Bust of Manolete kept in the bull-fighting Museum.

Pond in the Retiro overlooked by the statue of Alfonso XII.

THE RETIRO PARK

The Royal Preserve known as the Buen Retiro is one of Spain's loveliest parks. Philip IV ordered its construction in the orchard of the convent in the Monastery of San Jerónimo el Real, where the Spanish monarchs had always retired to since its foundation.

The Retiro covers an area of 143 hectares and is closed off by a valuable railing with twelve great gateways, the most important of them being those of the Plaza de la Independencia, Hernani, the Paseo de Coches and the Parterre. Situated in the middle of the capital to the right of the popular calle de Alcalá, El Retiro offers the gift of its beautiful gardens, its squares, ponds, walks, monuments, and its Crystal Palace now used for exhibitions.

Among the monuments inside the Retiro there are some that deserve special mention: the equestrian statue of Alfonso XII standing beside the great pool, sculpted by Mariano Benlliure; the Artichoke Fountain designed by Ventura Rodríguez towards the end of the XVIII century; also the monuments to the Fallen Angel, to Jacinto Verdaguer, Ramón de Campoamor, Chapí and to Cuba.

A close-up of the Crystal Palace of the Retiro, detail from the base of the monument to Alfonso XII, and a fine close-up of same.

Three beautiful views of the Rose Garden in the Retiro.

Monument to the Quintero brothers and a lovely shot of the Retiro Park.

Façade of the Army Museum, installed in the Salón de Reinos in the Royal Palace in the Retiro Park.

A view of the interesting collection of armour kept in the Army Museum.

◁ *View of one of the rooms in the Navy Museum.*

Façade of the Prado Museum, with San Jerónimo beside it.

THE PRADO MUSEUM

This famous art gallery is housed in a building constructed in 1785 from a design by the architect Juan de Villanueva, which was originally meant to be the home of the National Science Museum. Fernando VII took the decision of making it into an art gallery in 1819 and the museum ended up by taking the name of the noble avenue in which it was situated.

The building itself is in neoclassical style and in the shape of a parallelogram being 200 metres in length by 40 metres wide. The construction is of stone and brick with a greyish pink colour. At one side of the Prado Museum the outline of San Jerónimo el Real can be seen.

The front of the Prado is made up of a double gallery and in the centre is a doric peristyle. The lower gallery consists of fourteen half pointed arches and four which are straight. A cornice separates the lower gallery from the upper, which is held up by twenty eight ionic style columns. This majestic portico rests on half a dozen enormous columns and is in the centre of the two galleries.

When it was inaugurated on November 9th 1819, the Prado Museum had 311 works by Spanish painters belonging to the Royal Collection. At the present time it houses one of the most valuable collection of paintings in the world, with more than 3.000 works. Also interesting is the collection of sculptures, numbering more than 400 works. Also outstanding is the collection of objets d'art known as the Dauphin's Treasure, made up of the jewels and precious objects inherited

Las Meninas, *one of Velázquez's works of art.*

The Naked Maja, *one of Goya's most famous paintings.*

by Philip V from his father the Grand Dauphin of France.

The great school of Spanish painting is splendidly represented in the Prado Museum with 50 works by Velázquez, 50 by Ribera, 40 by Murillo, 33 by El Greco, 114 pictures and 50 engravings by Goya.

As regards foreign painting there are 661 Flemish masters, 435 Italian, 157 French, 138 Dutch, and an equally considerable number of German paintings. Particularly oustanding are 83 works by Rubens, 6 paintings and 50 drawings by Hieronymus Bosch, 40 works by Brueghel, 36 by Titian and 14 by Veronese. Some time ago numerous works by Aragonese, Catalan and Valencian primitives were incorporated into the Prado along with a valuable set of pictures from the baroque schools of Córdoba, Granada, Sevilla and Valencia.

The Romanesque frescoes — a mural decoration incorporated into a panting — from the hermitage of San Baudilio de Berlanga (Soria) and from the apse of the hermitage of Santa Cruz de Maderuelo (Segovia) are the most ancient of all the paintings on show in this Museum.

Among the Gothic paintings, two are specially noteworthy, — the altar-piece of Archbishop don Sancho de Rojas, by an unknown author, and the altar-piece of the Virgin and St. Francis, by Maestro Nicolás Francés.

From the XV century there are some tablets painted by Juan de Flandes and *El Salvador* (The Saviour) by Fernando Gallego, and from the XVI, *The Last Supper* by Juan de Juanes, *Virgin of the Souls* by Pedro Machuca, and *The Virgin and Child* by Morales.

The list of masterpieces of Spanish painting is truly extensive. In the Prado are several of the most famous pictures in the world. Among the Spanish ones mention must be made of *The Gentleman with his Hand at his Breast, The Baptism of Christ* and

The Children with the Shell, *a popular painting by Murillo.*

The Adoration of the Kings, *a canvas by Rubens.*

Andromeda freed by Perseus, *by Rubens.*

The Gentleman with his hand at his breast, *a portrait by El Greco.*

Christ bearing the Cross by El Greco; *St. Casilda* and *The Labours of Hercules* by Zurbarán; *The Martyrdom of St. Bartholomew* by Ribera; *Portrait of Isabel de Valois* by Pantoja; *Las Meninas, The Lances, Topers, Equestrian Portrait of Philip IV, Equestrian Portrait of the Count-Duke of Olivares,* and *Our Lord Crucified,* by Velázquez; *Self-Portrait,* and *Two Kings of Spain* by Alonso Cano; *Portrait of Philip II* and *The Infanta Isabel Clara Eugenia* by Sánchez Coello; *The Virgin and Child* by Claudio Coello; *Self-Portrait, The Immaculate Conception, The Good Shepherd* and *The Boys with the Shell* by Murillo; *Self-Portrait, The Naked Maja, The Family of Charles IV, Fernando VII* wearing a royal cloak, *The San Isidro Meadow, The Executions in the Moncloa* and the black paintings by Goya…

Among the most outstanding works by foreign artists are: *The Emperor Charles V on horseback, Self-Portrait* and *Venus enjoying Music* by Titian; *Portrait of a Cardinal* and *The Virgin with the Rose* by Rafael; *Micer Marsilio and his wife* by Lorenzo Lotto; *Self-Portrait* by Bassano; *The Gentleman with the Golden Chain* by Tintoretto; *Jesus and the Centurion* by Veronese; *David conquering Goliath* by Caravaggio; and practically all the work of Rubens, Hieronymus Bosch and Brueghel.

Statue to Velázquez at the entrance to the Prado Museum.

A delightful night time close-up of the Neptune fountain.

THE PASEO DEL PRADO

This is one of the loveliest and most characteristic avenues in Madrid, stretching from the Plaza de la Cibeles to the Plaza del Emperador Carlos V. The Paseo del Prado is shaded by many trees whose thick foliage lends the avenue an air of elegance and distinction.

On the other side of the Prado Museum, in the former Salón del Prado, where the smart people of the Romantic era used to meet, is the Neptune Fountain. This group sculpture was designed by Ventura Rodríguez and sculpted in white marble by Juan P. de Mena in 1782. The god Neptune, wearing a crown and with a trident in his hand stands on a carriage in the shape of a shell pulled by a team of horses. The Apollo Fountain is also to be found in the Paseo del Prado, this too was designed by Ventura Rodríguez and is also known as the Four Seasons.

A general view of the outside of the Prado Museum.

The front of the Congress of Deputies.

THE CONGRESS OF DEPUTIES

The Congress of Deputies is situated at the end of the Carrera de San Jerónimo close to the Neptune fountain. The building itself was designed by Narciso Pascual y Colomer. Work on it was begun in 1843 — its first stone being laid by Isabel II — and completed in 1850. The convent of the Holy Spirit formerly stood on this same site. The façade of the Congress building is made of granite except the sills, jambes, lintel, frieze and guards which are made from Colmenar stone; it has five very large columns holding up the triangular-shaped pediment. The two bronze lions flanking the main staircase were made by melting down cannon captured from the Moors during the African War in the XIX century. Congress is the legislative assembly of the Spanish monarchy.

The magnificent equestrian statue of Philip IV.

Plaza de Oriente, with the Royal Palace in the background.

THE PLAZA DE ORIENTE

Sited opposite the Royal Palace, this building is semicircular in shape. Vast in extension, it appears wider in the centre part with an impressive, beautifully kept flower bed. On either side of the square are tree filled gardens. In the centre, surrounded by fountain troughs, atop a high pedestal is the magnificent equestrian statue of Philip IV, one of the best pieces of sculpture adorning the capital of Spain. Designed by Velázquez and executed by Martínez-Montañés, Galileo and Pedro Tacca, the statue was placed in the Plaza de Oriente in the year 1884.

There are many statues surrounding the square, twice life size, sculpted in Colmenar stone and representing different kings of Spain. Formerly there were many trees around but these have been cut down to allow the view of the front of the Royal Palace and the fine statue of Philip IV to be seen from the Plaza de Oriente.

Almost opposite the Plaza de Oriente, at the other side of the calle de Bailén is the cathedral of La Almudena and the Sabatini Gardens at either side of the Royal Palace. From the square, in the distance, we can glimpse fragments of scenery under a luminous sky, slightly reminiscent of Velázquez.

The Plaza de Oriente is one of the most impressive spots in Madrid. Its vast space has been used on more than one occasion for mass demonstrations and it is also a place that invites one to a peaceful saunter.

The north side of the Royal Palace with the Sabatini gardens.

THE ROYAL PALACE

This palace is one of the most important monuments built in Madrid by the Borbons. A Borbon, Philip V began building the Royal Palace and another Borbon, Charles III completed it. The Royal Palace —also popularly known as the Palacio de Oriente— rises up on a hill situated on the left bank of the Manzanares. Occupying a vast extension of more than 150 metres on each side, it stands between the Plaza de Oriente and the Campo del Moro.

The Royal Palace occupies the same site as that formerly used by the old Alcázar of the House of Austria which was destroyed by fire on Christmas day 1734. Building work on the palace was undertaken in 1738 with the following architects taking part in its direction: Juvara, Sachetti, Ventura Rodríguez and

Campo del Moro, with the fountain of the Tritons.
(Reproduction authorized by the Patrimonio Nacional.)

View of the Plaza de Oriente and the Royal Palace.

Sabatini. The building was finished off twenty six years later.

The main entrance to the Royal Palace is in the Plaza de la Armería, on the side seen from the Plaza de Oriente. The architectural features on the outside (the building consists of four storeys) reveal a French influence, although inside there is a marked predominance of eighteenth century Italian taste. The Royal Palace is decorated with extraordinary richness. The majestic main staircase with its great marble steps has mural paintings by Giaquinto and a profusion of reliefs and sculptures. Of the many rooms in the palace, about fifty are open to the public and the influx of visitors has grown considerably since king Juan Carlos I acceded to the throne of Spain in 1975.

The first part that can be visited is the Salón de Alabarderos with its ceiling painted with motifs from the Aeneid by Tiepolo. Then there comes the Salón de las Columnas (the Hall of Columns) which was formerly a gala dining room. The two aforementioned rooms are rather like antechambers to the «cuarto del Rey» (King's room) composed of the three apartments inhabited by Charles III: the Saleta de Gasparini, its ceiling decorated with paintings by Mengs; the Gasparini antechamber where there are four portraits of Charles IV and María Luisa by Goya, and the Salón de Gasparini, a fine example of French rococo style.

The Salón de Gasparini leads to Charles III's bedroom and the Sala de Porcelana (Porcelaine Room) where

The Throne Room in the Royal Palace.
(Reproduction authorized by the Patrimonio Nacional.)

some fine sculptures by Bernini and lovely pieces from the Buen Retiro factory are kept.

Through the Yellow Room decorated with lovely vases, is an entrance into the Gala Dining Room, which is able to seat 145 people. Then there is the Music Room, the enormous chapel, the apartments of María Cristina, with paintings by the most famous XIX century masters, the Chambers of Mirrors, Tapestries and Weapons, all richly decorated, leading into the sumptuous Throne Room with its dome painted by Tiepolo. All this impressive part of the palace is luxuriously decorated and its wealth of art and treasures make it an outstanding museum in its own right.

Among the works of art to be seen in the Royal Palace, those worthy of special mention are, the fifteen magnificen tablets of the polyptic of the Catholic Queen, works by Juan de Flandes; the fine portrait of Duke Philip the Good of Burgundy, painted by Van der Weyden; the *Road to Calvary* by Hieronymus Bosch; another painting on the same theme by Miguel de Coxcie; *Salome* by Caravaggio; *Head of a Woman,* a miniature painting of the Count-Duke de Olivares, and a study of a white horse, all of them works by Velázquez; the portrait of Don Juan de Austria on horseback by Ribera; *Making Gunpowder in the Sierra Tardienta* and *Making Bullets,* two pictures by Goya. The list of valuable paintings in the Royal Palace would be interminable considering there are works by Rubens, Zurbarán, Bassano, Watteau,

The Gasparini Room, decorated by the painter of that name.

(Reproduction authorized by the Patrimonio Nacional.)

Bayeu, Palmarolli, Houasse, Vicente López, Maella, Madrazo, Sorolla and Cecilio Pla.

The collections of precious metal objects, royal capes, religious garments and royal china from different periods and reigns are of inestimable value both from the artistic and strictly historical and documentary point of view.

Also of great interest is the collection of clocks of many different periods, styles and types installed in the so-called Salón del Cine decorated in Renaissance style.

Inside the Museum which is the Royal Palace are other fascinating objects. Particularly outstanding is the collection of tapestries considered one of the best and most valuable in the world. There are magnificent pieces of cloth woven in Brussels in the XV and XVI centuries with silver and gold thread, lovely colours and undoubted beauty.

The Sala de la Princesa can also be considered a genuine museum with its lovely green canopy embroidered in embossed gold, a real jewel of the Empire style, with the coats of arms of Fernando VII and his fourth wife, Queen María Cristina de Borbón. The Music Museum is also worth seeing with its splendid

The sumptuous State Dining Room in the Royal Palace.
(Reproduction authorized by the Patrimonio Nacional.)

collection of violins and violas, the Stradivarius quintet —specially made for the Spanish court when Philip V was king—, harps, guitars, pianos, scores and different documents apertaining to reknowned composers and artists in the sphere of music.

Close by is the ancient Royal Library which is reached through the main courtyard. The Library has 24 rooms and houses a valuable collection of more than 300.000 volumes, with maps, manuscripts and now unobtainable editions of books printed in the XV century. Among its treasures are original collections of Books of Hours from the XV century, many incunabulars, manuscripts relating to the history of America, and books with rich Spanish and foreign bindings.

Another curious museum in the Royal Palace is that of the Royal Apothec or Royal Pharmaceutical Office with its reproduction of a XVII century alchemist's laboratory. The two rooms comprising the Apothec are furnished with cupboards filled with the original procelaine jars, glass vessels and the most varied and evocative selection of old apparatus and medical and pharmacological tools. There is also a valuable specialized library, with more than 3.000 volumes, among them unique publications and recipe books

A general view of the Royal Palace in Madrid.

made for the kings, with the formulae for preparing different medicines.

Of extraordinary interest is the Royal Armoury which is considered the best collection in the world, of its type. The Royal Armoury consists of two adjacent rooms in the Royal Palace. Founded by Philip II with the basic objective of collecting and preserving arms that had belonged to his father and to himself. The Royal Armoury was installed in its present location in 1893. The content of the Arms Museum is as varied as it is valuable. Among the vast amount of pieces kept in the Royal Armoury, the most outstanding is the impressive armour and original harnesses that belonged to Charles I of Spain, Philip II, Philip the Handsome, Ferdinand and Isabella, Boabdil, Don Sebastian of Portugal, Maximilian of Austria, Prince Charles, and all the kings of the Houses of Austria and Borbon. There are also many valuable and histotically interesting trophies and souvernirs evoking the great battles fought by the Spaniards at crucial moments in world history: Lepanto, Las Navas, Pavía, Mühlberg...

Finally the Carriage Museum must be mentioned. Its main content has come from the former Royal Stables and is now installed in the Campo del Moro in a new building surrounded by fine gardens and ponds. This is an excellent collection of light carriages, berlines, coaches, landeaux, victorias and other types of vehicle used by the kings of Spain between the XVI and XX centuries. The Carriage Museum also has a varied collection of saddles, harnesses, servants' livery, and tapestries.

Façade of the Royal Theatre, with the statue of Philip IV.

THE ROYAL THEATRE

This building is situated between the Oriente and Isabel II squares, in the same place where the Coliseum of the Caños del Peral once stood, which was demolished in 1818 when it was already in ruins. That same year work was undertaken on the building of the Royal Theatre, under the direction of the architect Antonio López Aguado. Not long after, the work was interrupted and begun again between 1822 and 1824 under the direction of Custodio Moreno. There was a further interruption of a decade, then work was continued from 1835 to 1837, again paralysed for thirteen years until the theatre was finally inaugurated on November 19th 1850 with a performance of *La Favorita* by Donizetti.

The Royal Theatre consisted of five storeys with a portico and stone arches opening onto the Plaza de Oriente, while the rear part looked onto the Plaza de Isabel II in the centre of which stands the statue of the Queen. In former times there were staircases on either side of the portico which were only used by the king and queen and members of the Royal Family. The side facing the Plaza de Oriente was decorated with sculptures, reliefs of musical allegories, busts of Mozart, Moratín, Garcilaso de la Vega, Rossini, Iriarte and Meléndez Valdés, the likenesses of Calderón de la Barca, Lope de Vega and the attic topped by a coat of arms. The Royal Theatre is now the seat of the Royal Conservatory and houses the schools of music, song, ballet and dramatic art, also a large sumptuously decorated concert hall.

The Amusement Park in the Casa de Campo.

THE CASA DE CAMPO

This large park with a wood and gardens is the oldest in Madrid. It is situated between the roads to Extramadura and Corunna, stretching over to the other side of the Manzanares. Large in area, some 1,747 hectares, it is surrounded by a brick wall. This was the former garden of the kings, and now it is Madrid's loveliest park.

The Casa de Campo is in the shape of an irregular polygon and is reached through seven gateways, la Puerta del Río, the main entrance, la Puerta del Castillo, la Puerta de Medianil, de Rodejos, de Aravaca, de la Venta and del Angel. The fine statue of Philip III on horseback — now in the centre of the

Plaza Mayor — stood, until 1848, opposite this main gateway to the Casa de Campo.

This vast park was created by Philip II in 1562 when he acquired a large amount of land from Fadrique Vargas with the idea that it should become part of the Royal Wood. Later on the Casa de Campo was enlarged and improved with lands by Fernando VI, Charles III, Isabel II, and the mother of Alfonso XIII, doña María Cristina de Hapsburgo. What was until then known as the Royal Wood became the Casa de Campo on April 20th 1931 when the park was given to the people of Madrid.

The Casa de Campo, this green belt in the centre of Madrid, is one of the most delightful and popular parts of the city during the summer months. People

Four views of the
Amusement Park in the
Casa de Campo, among
them the tower-top
restaurant known as the
«Flying Saucer» and the
busy Avenida de
Surtidores.

Panoramic view of the Casa de Campo.

Several views of the Zoo in the Casa de Campo.

wander happily about under the shade of the many trees or on the shores of the lovely lake, and fill this large and beautiful park with their enjoyment.

In former times, in this enourmous park, ten times larger than the famous Bois de Boulogne in Paris, was the first race course for horse racing in Madrid, a pond for ice-skating, clay pigeon shooting, numerous fountains, hunting pavilions and many other buildings. Several of these curious buildings in the Casa de Campo have been preserved, among them «La Torrecilla», «La Sala de las Burlas», «La Casa-Administración», «El Laberinto», and «La Faisanera Vieja».

The impressive lake is especially noteworthy among the many marvels in the park, it has a quay for pleasure launches and boats, giving the impression that Madrid is on the sea shore. Along the lake side are many comfortable picnicking places.

There is also a magnificent Amusement Park in the Casa de Campo, an auditorium, restaurants and dance halls, making it an attractive place for visitors. A further attraction is the cable car which goes from the city to the Casa de Campo. (Its terminus is in the calle del Pintor Rosales).

The Zoo with its many animals is a fine place for children; some years ago this was in the Retiro, but now it occupies a more suitable establishment in the Casa de Campo; there is also an area set aside for the Feria del Campo, an important competition taking place every two years.

A night time view of the Puerta de Toledo.

A close-up of San Francisco el Grande by Sabatini. ▷

THE PUERTA DE TOLEDO

This is sited in the centre of the square between the end of the calle de Toledo and the beginning of the old Paseo de los Ocho Hilos. The Puerta de Toledo used to be the gateway into Madrid coming from Andalusia. Work on its construction began in 1813 under the direction of the architect Antonio Aguado, but this was interrupted for several years and the gateway was not completed until 1827. The monument consists of a central half pointed archway of considerable dimensions with two straight doors at either side, lower and smaller in size. On top of the attic above the

cornice with ionic fluted pilastres is a group sculpture flanked by the figures of Arts and Genius. The Puerta de Toledo is somewhat neoclassical in style with baroque additions.

Neart to the Puerta de Toledo is the elegant bridge of the same name which was completed in 1732 consisting of nine half pointed archways spanning the river Manzanares. Architecturally the Puerta de Toledo is predominantly baroque in style with a pair of niches in the centre of the balcony, one on the right, and the other on the left, decorated with a statue of San Isidro, and another opposite, with a statue of his wife, Santa María de la Cabeza.

View of El Rastro, with the statue of Cascorro.   *Several views of the popular market El Rastro.* ▷

EL RASTRO

One of the most popular and picturesque scenes of Madrid. A multicoloured market, where the most unusual cast off objects are bought and sold, clothes, furniture, and antiques from the most contrasting parts of the city. This unique auction centre is to be found in an old part of Madrid that begins in the popular Plaza de Cascorro, stretching along the irregular streets close by the Ribera de Curtidores, the main thoroughfare of El Rastro.

You can buy almost anything from the open air stalls of El Rastro, from paintings and engravings to books, costume jewellery, car parts, old blunderbuses, ball point pens and used shoes. The antique shops are also filled with a wide variety of strange objects.

Romantic Museum: the pistol with which Larra committed suicide.

ROMANTIC MADRID

This was in the area which, due to the expansion that took place under the monarchs of the House of Austria, extended and is still extending around the Puerta del Sol and the Plaza Mayor, along the calle de Atocha to the Paseo del Prado. The characteristic streets of romantic Madrid are those of el Prado (where the Atheneum stands), León, Cervantes, and Lope de Vega. There were many cafés in the streets near to the Puerta del Sol where the most famous figures of romanticism in Madrid, such as Larra, Espronceda and Ventura de la Vega used to meet. One of the most famous literary coteries in Madrid during the Romantic period was the one known as «El Parnasillo» that met in the café del Príncipe.

The atmosphere of Madrid at the turn of the century is reflected in the rooms of the Romantic Museum situated in the calle de San Mateo, in the former palace of the Marqués de la Vega-Inclán. One of the most frequently visited rooms in this museum is the one dedicated to Mariano José de Larra, where objects belonging to the writer, including the very pistol with which he committed suicide, have been kept.

The Contemporary Poets, a painting by Esquivel.

One of the rooms in the Romantic Museum.

The baroque portal of the Municipal Library and Museum.

THE ARCHAEOLOGICAL MUSEUM

Situated at the beginning of the calle de Serrano, next to the Puerta de Alcalá, this museum was created by Royal Decree in 1867 by Isabel II. At first the National Archaeological Museum was housed in the Casino de la Reina in the calle de Embajadores. Later, on July 5th 1895, the dependencies of the Museum were transferred to the palace built for the National Libraries and Museums. Between the years 1954 and 1964 the building was reconstructed and in 1964 the splendid reproductions of the paleolithic paintings of Altamira (Santander) were installed in a specially conditioned basement at the entrance to the garden which serves as an open air vestibule for the Archaeological Museum.

XII century Romanesque capital from the Monastery of Santa María (Aguilar de Campoo).

Votive crown of Recesvinto. (Guarrazar, Toledo.)

Entrance to the National Archaeological Museum.

View of the Plaza de Colón.

The first contents of the museum were a valuable collection of coins — about 20.000 — that had belonged to Philip V, and some pieces of differing origin that used to be kept in the basement of the National Science Museum.

At the present time the Archaeological Museum consists of 30 spacious rooms and two large courtyards with a glass skylight. Among the museum's possessions composed of valuable collections of prehistoric and historic objects in ceramic, coins and royal seals, the following are specially outstanding: the famous Dama de Elche, the original Iberian bull, androcephalous known as «La Bicha de Balazote», a XIII century Limoges coffre, the «Gran Oferente del Cerro de los Santos», a beautiful Roman agate goblet, the Romanesque portal of the Burgos Monastery of San Pedro de Arlanza, the decorative columns of San Pelayo de Antealtares, the sarcophagus of Husillos (Palencia), the Iberian relief and Celtic diadem of Osuna, the lamp of the Alhambra mosque, the ivory curcifix of don Fernando I and doña Sancha, and the «Diosa de Baza», found some years ago in the province of Granada.

Mention must also be made of the invaluable collection of coins, more than 200,000 from every period and country; decorative porcelaine from Sèvres, Saxony, Wedgewood, Vienna, Urbino, Alcora, Buen Retiro, and La Moncloa; the large collection of popular ceramics; the collection of Greek and Etruscan vases; the sarcophagi from far off times; the collection of votive lamps, Iberian sculptures and Greek, Roman and Pompeyan mosaics.

*Discovery Gardens in the Plaza de Colón,
and underground walks decorated with
paintings on subjects related to Columbus.*

A general view of the Temple of Debod.

Façade of the Libraries and Museums building. ▷

THE EGYPTIAN TEMPLE OF DEBOD

This temple, whose site in Egypt was submerged by the waters after the construction of the Assuan dam on the Nile, was built 25 centuries ago.

Dismantled stone by stone and brought to Spain, it was faithfully assembled, respecting its original structure in the gardens of the former barracks of La Montaña. In its present location the Temple of Debod is surrounded by palm trees and exotic flowers.

THE NATIONAL LIBRARY

Installed on the first floor of the Palace of National Libraries and Museums, the library is reached through a spacious hall in white marble decorated with the sculptures of Menéndez Pelayo, a work by Coullaut Valera, of Isabel II sculpted by Piquer, and sculptures of other notables.

The National Library is one of the most important in the world. Its original collection came from the Royal Library, founded in 1712 by Philip V, and from books preserved in the Royal Alcázar. Now the library has more than five million books, manuscripts, incunabulars —2.500— leaflets, prints, engravings and magazines. Outstanding among the collections in the National Library is the codex of the Poema del Cid and the Cervantine collection consisting of more than 3,000 editions of *The Quixote* in more than thirty languages, some of them beautifully illustrated.

The National Library consists of different sections, among these the most remarkable are, the General Section, the Unusual Section, the Manuscripts, Fine Arts, Music and Record Library.

They still say that fish is dear, *a painting by Sorolla.*

THE MUSEUM OF CONTEMPORARY ART

This museum is installed in a modern skyscraper in the Avenida de Juan de Herrera, in the University City. Founded at the end of the XIX century, it was first known as the Museum of Contemporary Art, and a little later, the National Museum of Modern Art. Later, the Museum of Contemporary Art was created, which in 1968 was known as the Spanish Museum of Con-

temporary Art. Until a few years ago, this museum was installed in the National Palace of Libraries and Museums.

Its rooms offer the interesting panorama of the evolution of Spanish painting and sculpture during this century. Among the paintings it houses, the following are of note: those by Anglada Camarasa, Joaquín Sorolla, Romero de Torres, Gutiérrez Solana, Darío Regoyos, Isidro Nonell, Rusiñol, Zuloaga, Vázquez Díaz, Picasso, Miró, and Dalí.

Winter Morning, *by Ricardo Baroja kept in the Museum of Contemporary Art.*

The Van, *a painting by Ricardo Baroja also on show in the Museum of Contemporary Art.*

A partial view of the Paseo de la Castellana.

THE AVENUE OF LA CASTELLANA

The Avenues of Recoletos and the Castellana are similar in structure and constitute a harmonious addition to the city. The Paseo de Recoletos stretches from the Plaza de la Cibeles to Colón where the Castellana begins, ending in the Plaza de San Juan de la Cruz. The Paseo de la Castellana is one of the loveliest and most popular avenues in Madrid. Flanked by shady trees and small palaces, it has an aristocratic air. In spite of the intensive modernization of Madrid, the Castellana has preserved its genuine personality and all the typical enchantment of former times when the capital of Spain was not yet the large city it is today.

Bridge over the Avenida de la Paz and la Castellana.

An impressive close-up of the Plaza de Castilla.

Beyond the Paseo de la Castellana, a new dynamic part of the city has grown up, epitomizing the vast expansion of Madrid especially during the 1950s. This ultramodern area begins with the new Ministries and reaches the height of ultramodern architecture in the large buildings stretching out beyond, great blocks of flats, banks, offices, American bars... A very different world, essentially, from that of La Castellana, an impressive link with the Madrid of yesteryear.

A view of one of the avenues of modern Madrid.

*Partial view
of the Paseo
de
Recoletos.*

View of the dynamic Gran Vía.

The Telephone Exchange, between the Gran Vía and Fuencarral.

A fine close-up of the Paseo de Recoletos.

View of the Plaza de San Juan de la Cruz and the National Health Building of La Paz.

A view of
the Gran
Vía.

◁ *A splendid close-up of the Plaza del Callao.*

The Plaza del Callao and Gran Vía.

THE PLAZA DEL CALLAO

This square is located between the Gran Vía and the streets of Preciados and el Carmen. This is one of the most popular squares with the densent pedestrian traffic in Madrid. The Plaza del Callao is an important nerve centre as regards bus stops, and is literally surrounded by hotels, cinemas, cafés, and department stores. In the square are the large buildings of the Press Palace and the Callao, Capital and Rex Cinemas. The section of the calle de Preciados leading from the Plaza del Callao to the Puerta del Sol is filled with department stores and commercial establishments which are always full of people. The calle del Carmen, running parallel to the calle Preciados is similar in type.

Close to Callao, only separated by two small streets, in the colourful bustle of the square, is the important Museum of the Descalzas Reales, belonging to the convent of the same name. The quiet peaceful place where it is situated still preserves a certain XVI century air, contrasting markedly with the almost tumultuous dynamism of the Plaza del Callao. In the Convent of the Descalzas Reales, founded by a daughter of the Emperor Charles V, doña María de Austria, and a daughter of «El Españoleto» were nuns. The museum, opened to the public in 1961, has some valuable paintings by Titian, Zurbarán, Sánchez Coello and some primitive artists. Also of interest are the frescoes by Nani, tapestries based on original cartoons by Rubens, and the collections of relics and jewels.

A night time view of the Plaza de España.

THE PLAZA DE ESPAÑA

After the Plaza del Callao, going down the Gran Vía, comes the Plaza de España. The first objects that appear are the shapes of the two skyscrapers known as Edificio España and Torre de Madrid, having 26 and 34 storeys respectively, which in a way makes the wide expanse of the square look smaller. Nonetheless, the Plaza de España is one of the most popular scenes of Madrid and one which constantly appears on post cards and the like.

In the centre stands a monument to Don Miguel de Cervantes, and in front of the statue of the eminent writer, his beloved immortal creations Don Quixote and Sancho Panza are depicted on horseback in bronze. The Plaza de España is a busy area and it is usual to see visitors taking photos especially of the statue. Beyond the square are areas of attractive green countryside.

However, this popular square occupies a privileged position as it is practically in the centre of Madrid and therefore close to the Casa de Campo and the Parque del Oeste.

Leading from the Plaza de España is the elegant calle Princesa which ends around the area of the University City. Number 22 on this street is the Palacio de Liria, the residence of the Duchess of Alba. In this aristocratic mansion standing in a magnificent park, are some valuable paintings by Velázquez, El Greco, Goya, Titian, Rembrandt, Rubens and Van Dyck.

*Monument
to Cervantes
in the centre
of the Plaza
de España.*

Close-up of the statues of Don Quixote and Sancho Panza.

The elegant calle de la Princesa.

The Plaza de la Moncloa, with the Air Ministry on the right.

Close-up of the Arco de la Victoria. ▷

PLAZA DE LA MONCLOA

In former times this was known as the Plaza de Cánovas del Castillo. Now the Plaza de la Moncloa with its spacious modern structure, is a nerve centre of the attractive Argüelles district where the carefree student population strolls about. The streets of Fernando el Católico, Fernández de los Ríos, Isaac Peral and Moret begin in the square and the calle Princesa ends there.

The Ministry of Aviation building designed on balanced Escorial lines stands in the Plaza de la Moncloa and close by are the Institute of Hispanic Culture and the America Museum, which, under the perceptive direction of Martínez Barbeito, have succeeded in making important collections of idols, cloth, ceramic, and other decorative objects from pre- and postcolumbnian American art. The Arco de Triunfo is beside the Plaza de la Moncloa, opening onto the University City.

Several views of the lovely Parque del Oeste, one of the largest green belts in Madrid.

The Torch Bearers, *by Ana Vaughan Hyatt.*

Partial view of the University City.

THE UNIVERSITY CITY

Stretching from the Moncloa and bordering on the Puerta de Hierro and the woods of El Pardo, the building of the University City was first thought of by Alfonso XIII to commemorate his Silver Jubilee. The original project underwent several modifications, until it finally became one of the largest University campuses in Europe. The University City includes colleges of residence, faculties, and other dependencies. In front of the Medical Faculty is the statue to «The Torch Bearers» by Ana V. Hyatt.

MADRID AND SPORT

Madrid has magnificent sports installations of every kind. As regards football, undoubtedly the most popular sport among the people of Madrid, mention must be made of two splendid stadiums, the Bernabeu, owned by Real Madrid and the Vicente Calderón (Manzanares) belonging to Madrid Athletic. These two clubs have different sections devoted to other sports. There are also many municipal sports in-

The magnificent Madrid Athletic stadium.

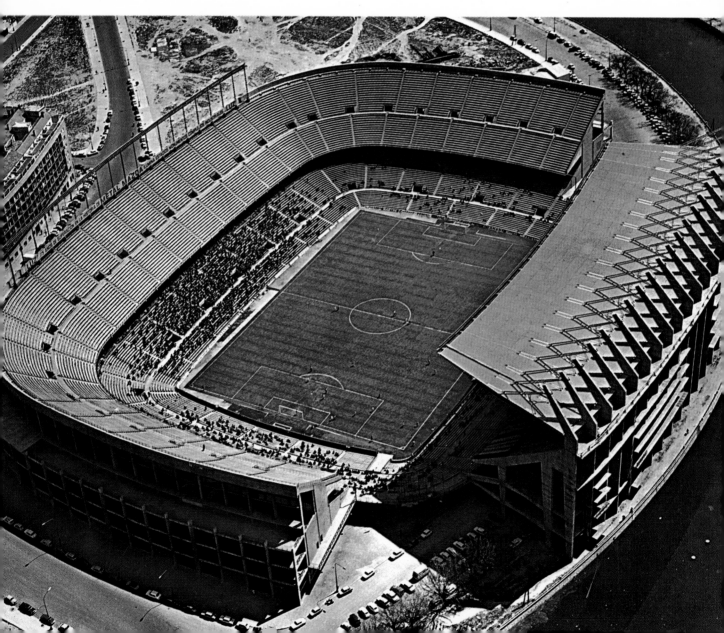

The enormous Santiago Bernabeu stadium of Real Madrid.

stallations, among them the vast Sports Palace, the scene of unforgettable sporting events.

Another sport that enjoys great esteem in Madrid is horse racing which takes place in the Hippodrome of the Zarzuela, close by the University City which also has its own sports grounds.

Not far from the Hippodrome in the residential area of Puerta de Hierro, there are a large number of clubs where tennis, polo and golf can be played, with swimming and clay-pigeon shooting facilities too.

About half a dozen golf clubs are open throughout the year and lessons are given on how to play this elegant game.

Every day there is dog racing at the Madrid dog racing track (El Canódromo Madrileño) situated in the Vía Carpetana (Carabanchel). The Basque pelota game also attracts many enthusiasts and there are interesting games every afternoon at the Frontón Madrid, in the calle del Dr. Cortezo n.º 10. Car racing is particularly important; these races are valid for the world championship and take place at the Jarama race track.

Puerta de Hierro, built during the reign of Fernando VI.

The Zarzuela Palace, the residence of Their Majesties the King and Queen of Spain.
(Reproduction authorized by the Patrimonio Nacional.)

THE ZARZUELA PALACE

Sited in a position of great natural beauty, next to woods and the El Pardo hill, both El Pardo and La Zarzuela were formerly impressive royal estates. The Zarzuela Palace is in a way part of the scenery of the areas occupied by the University City and has the mountains as a magnificent back cloth. The Palace of La Zarzuela was built acoording to the designs of the architects Juan Gómez de Mora, and Alonso Carbonell, maestro Juan de Aguilar having directed the work. Formerly a pleasure residence of the kings, it was destroyed during the Civil War and completely rebuilt in 1960. It is an elegant functional modern mansion and has now been converted into the official residence of Their Majesties King Don Juan Carlos I and Queen Sofia; it is furnished in good taste but with no ostentation as befits its royal inhabitants.

The Zarzuela is surrounded by well kept gardens and from its simple, sober appearance — pinkish walls, slate roof, and low construction — nobody would say, if they didn't know beforehand, that it was here where a head of State and a king of Spain resided. Nevertheless it is in the Zarzuela Palace where H. M. Juan Carlos I receives all the Spanish and foreign visitors who call on him.

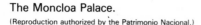

The Moncloa Palace.
(Reproduction authorized by the Patrimonio Nacional.)

The colossal cross on the Valley of the Fallen.
(Reproduction authorized by the Patrimonio Nacional.)

The front of the El Pardo Palace.
(Reproduction authorized by the Patrimonio Nacional.)

THE MONCLOA PALACE

Situated five kilometres along the motor way to Corunna, close to El Pardo, the Moncloa Palace is surrounded by gardens and trees, on a rise not far from los Viveros de la Villa. Built in the XVII century, it was later altered and its anteroom was even decorated by Goya. The residence of the French Marshall Murat in 1808, it became state property during the second half of the XIX century. Destroyed during the Civil War, it was later restored and extended under the direction of the architect Diego Méndez. Now it is used as the official residence of the Prime Minister.

THE PALACE OF EL PARDO

At a distance of some 15 kilometres from Madrid, it is surrounded by a fine wood which was used for hunting and pleasure by the kings of Castile. Charles V built a palace in the same place as that formerly occupied by a hunting lodge in the time of Enrique III, this was later altered on many occasions and in the reign of Charles III, Sabatini made it what it is today. The Palace of El Pardo was the official residence of General Franco during the time he was Chief of State; it now houses an interesting well-filled museum showing aspects of his military and political career.

A view of the Monastery of San Lorenzo of El Escorial.
(Reproduction authorized by the Patrimonio Nacional.)

THE VALLEY OF THE FALLEN

This monument is 58 kilometres from Madrid and stands in Cuelgamuros, a high area between El Escorial and the Guadarrama. Built on the orders of General Franco who has been buried in the church of the Valley of the Fallen since 1975, it is in memory of the soldiers from both sides who died in the three years of Civil War.

The stone cross dominating the basilica measures 150 m. in height and is said to weigh 181.740 tons. The front of the church occupies one side of the esplanade and its grandiose style is in contrast with the natural grandeur of the mountains.

EL ESCORIAL

Forty kilometres from Madrid stands the Monastery of San Lorenzo de El Escorial. This architectural marvel was built on the orders of Philip II to commemorate the Spanish victory in the Battle of San Quintín, and at the same time destined to be the Royal Tomb of the House of Austria. Work was begun in 1563 under the direction of Juan Bautista de Toledo, and completed in 1584 under Juan de Herrera.

El Escorial is undoubtedly one of the most justly famed monuments in the world. There are some fine artistic treasures stored inside and the library has more than 40.000 valuable volumes.

THE ROYAL PALACE OF ARANJUEZ

The lovely town of Aranjuez is situated some 47 kilometres from Madrid in the centre of a fertile valley filled with light, at the confluence of the Jarama and the Tagus. Apart from the natural beauty of the countryside, Aranjuez holds the attraction of the Royal Palace and its wonderful gardens. The palace was built at the beginning of the XV century and later altered during the reigns of Philip II, Philip V, Charles III and other monarchs, it is richly furnished in XVIII century taste and has valuable collections of paintings, with works by Lucas Jordán, Mengs, and other masters, marbles, bronzes, sumptuous objects, and clothes from past centuries.

The so-called Casa de Marinos is also most interesting, this is where the Museum of the Royal Boats is housed, and where besides the boats which give their name to the museum, several small cannon, fishing tackle from different periods, uniforms, engravings and historical documents are kept. Special mention must be made of the Casita del Labrador, two kilometres from the Royal Palace, built on the orders of Charles IV, it has a valuable museum containing porcelaine, lamps, clocks, furniture, sculpture, bronzes, agates, and other decorative pieces.

A lovely spot in the Royal Country Residence of Aranjuez.

Contents

That ancient part of history which is Spain is often referred to as "the bull's skin", because that is the shape of Spain on the map. The aim of this book is to present a detailed and comprehensive picture of a fragment of that "bull's skin", and to help this it includes a number of spectacular photographs. The Editor will be well satisfied if he has succeeded in giving you a deeper and better knowledge of Spain.

Collection ALL EUROPE

	Spanish	French	English	German	Italian	Catalan	Dutch	Swedish	Portuguese	Japanese	Arab
1 ANDORRA	■	■	■	■	□	■	□	□	□	■	□
2 LISBON	■	■	■	■	□	□	□	□	■	□	□
3 LONDON	■	■	■	■	□	□	□	□	□	■	□
4 BRUGES	■	■	■	■	□	□	■	□	□	□	□
5 PARIS	■	■	■	■	■	□	□	□	□	■	□
6 MONACO	■	■	■	■	■	□	□	□	□	□	□
7 VIENNA	■	■	■	■	■	□	■	□	■	■	■
8 NICE	■	■	■	■	■	□	□	□	□	□	□
9 CANNES	■	■	■	■	■	□	□	□	□	□	□
10 ROUSSILLON	■	■	■	■	□	■	□	□	■	□	□
11 VERDUN	■	■	■	■	□	□	□	□	□	□	□
12 THE TOWER OF LONDON	■	■	■	■	□	□	□	□	□	□	□
13 ANTWERP	■	■	■	■	□	□	■	□	□	□	□
14 WESTMINSTER ABBEY	■	■	■	■	■	□	□	□	□	□	□
15 THE SPANISH RIDING SCHOOL IN VIENNA	■	■	■	■	■	□	□	□	□	□	□
16 FATIMA	■	■	■	■	□	□	□	□	■	□	□
17 WINDSOR CASTLE	■	■	■	■	■	□	□	□	□	■	□
18 THE OPAL COAST	□	■	■	□	□	□	□	□	□	□	□
19 COTE D'AZUR	■	■	■	■	■	□	□	□	□	□	□
20 AUSTRIA	■	■	■	■	■	□	□	□	□	□	□
21 LOURDES	■	■	■	■	□	□	□	□	□	□	□
22 BRUSSELS	■	■	■	■	□	□	■	□	□	□	□

Collection ALL AMERICA

	Spanish	French	English	German	Italian	Catalan	Dutch	Swedish	Portuguese	Japanese	Arab
1 PUERTO RICO	■	□	■	□	□	□	□	□	□	□	□
2 SANTO DOMINGO	■	□	■	□	□	□	□	□	□	□	□

Collection ALL AFRICA

	Spanish	French	English	German	Italian	Catalan	Dutch	Swedish	Portuguese	Japanese	Arab
1 MOROCCO	■	■	■	■	□	□	□	□	□	□	■

Collection ART IN SPAIN

	Spanish	French	English	German	Italian	Catalan	Dutch	Swedish	Portuguese	Japanese	Arab
1 PALAU DE LA MUSICA CATALANA (Catalan Palace of Music)	■	■	■	■	□	■	□	□	□	□	□
2 GAUDI	■	■	■	■	■	■	□	□	□	□	□
3 PRADO MUSEUM I (Spanish Painting)	■	■	■	■	■	□	□	□	□	■	□
4 PRADO MUSEUM II (Foreign Painting)	■	■	■	■	■	□	□	□	□	□	□
5 THE ROOF-BOSSES OF THE CATHEDRAL OF GERONA	■	□	□	□	□	□	□	□	□	□	□
6 THE CASTLE OF XAVIER	■	□	□	□	□	□	□	□	□	□	□
7 THE ROMANESQUE STYLE IN SPAIN	■	■	■	■	□	□	□	□	□	□	□
8 SPANISH CASTLES	■	■	■	■	□	□	□	□	□	□	□
9 THE CATHEDRALS OF SPAIN	■	■	■	■	□	□	□	□	□	□	□
10 THE CATHEDRAL OF GERONA	■	■	■	■	□	□	□	□	□	□	□
11 GRAN TEATRO DEL LICEO DE BARCELONA (The Great Opera House)	■	■	■	■	■	■	□	□	□	□	□
12 THE ROMANESQUE STYLE IN CATALONIA	■	■	■	■	□	□	□	□	□	□	□
13 LA RIOJA: ART TREASURES AND WINE-GROWING RESOURCES	■	■	■	■	□	□	□	□	□	□	□
14 PICASSO	■	■	■	■	□	□	□	□	□	□	□
15 THE BAROQUE STYLE IN SPAIN	■	■	■	■	□	□	□	□	□	□	□
16 ROMAN REMAINS IN SPAIN	■	■	■	■	□	□	□	□	□	□	□
17 THE GOTHIC STYLE IN SPAIN	■	■	■	■	□	□	□	□	□	□	□
18 THE WINES OF CATALONIA	■	■	■	■	□	□	□	□	□	□	□
19 THE ALHAMBRA AND THE GENERALIFE	■	■	■	■	□	□	□	□	□	□	□
20 GRANADA AND THE ALHAMBRA (ARAB AND MAURESQUE MONUMENTS OF CORDOVA, SEVILLE AND GRANADA)	■	□	□	□	□	□	□	□	□	□	□

Collection ALL SPAIN

	Spanish	French	English	German	Italian	Catalan	Dutch	Swedish	Portuguese	Japanese	Arab
1 ALL MADRID	■	■	■	■	■	□	□	□	□	■	□
2 ALL BARCELONA	■	■	■	■	■	■	□	□	□	□	□
3 ALL SEVILLE	■	■	■	■	■	□	□	□	□	■	□
4 ALL MAJORCA	■	■	■	■	■	□	□	□	□	□	□
5 ALL THE COSTA BRAVA	■	■	■	□	□	□	□	□	□	□	□
6 ALL MALAGA and the Costa del Sol	■	■	■	■	□	□	□	□	□	□	□
7 ALL THE CANARY ISLANDS I, Lanzarote and Fuerteventura	■	■	■	■	□	□	■	■	□	□	□
8 ALL CORDOBA	■	■	■	■	■	□	□	□	□	□	□
9 ALL GRANADA	■	■	■	■	■	□	□	□	■	□	□
10 ALL VALENCIA	■	■	■	■	■	□	□	□	□	□	□
11 ALL TOLEDO	■	■	■	■	■	□	□	□	□	□	■
12 ALL SANTIAGO and the Rías Bajas	■	■	■	■	□	□	□	□	□	□	□
13 ALL IBIZA and Formentera	■	■	■	■	□	□	□	□	□	□	□
14 ALL CADIZ and the Costa de la Luz	■	■	■	■	□	□	□	□	□	□	□
15 ALL MONTSERRAT	■	■	■	■	□	□	□	□	□	□	□
16 ALL SANTANDER and the Costa Esmeralda	■	■	■	□	□	□	□	□	□	□	□
17 ALL THE CANARY ISLANDS II, Tenerife, La Palma, Gomera, Hierro	■	■	■	■	□	□	■	■	□	□	□
18 ALL PEÑISCOLA	■	■	■	■	□	□	□	□	□	□	□
19 ALL SITGES	■	■	■	■	□	□	□	□	□	□	□
20 ALL BURGOS, Covarrubias and Santo Domingo de Silos	■	■	■	■	□	□	□	□	□	□	□
21 ALL ALICANTE and the Costa Blanca	■	■	■	■	□	■	□	□	□	□	□
22 ALL NAVARRA	■	■	■	■	□	□	□	□	□	□	□
23 ALL LERIDA Province and Pyrenees	■	■	■	■	□	■	□	□	□	□	□
24 ALL SEGOVIA and Province	■	■	■	■	□	□	□	□	□	□	□
25 ALL SARAGOSSA and Province	■	■	■	■	□	□	□	□	□	□	□
26 ALL SALAMANCA and Province	■	■	■	■	□	□	□	□	□	■	□
27 ALL AVILA and Province	■	■	■	■	□	□	□	□	□	□	□
28 ALL MINORCA	■	■	■	■	□	□	□	□	□	□	□
29 ALL SAN SEBASTIAN and Province	■	■	■	■	□	□	□	□	□	□	□
30 ALL ASTURIAS	■	■	■	■	□	□	□	□	□	□	□
31 ALL CORUNNA and the Rías Altas	■	■	■	■	□	□	□	□	□	□	□
32 ALL TARRAGONA and Province	■	■	■	■	□	□	□	□	□	□	□
33 ALL MURCIA and Province	■	■	■	■	□	□	□	□	□	□	□
34 ALL VALLADOLID and Province	■	■	■	■	□	□	□	□	□	□	□
35 ALL GIRONA and Province	■	■	■	■	□	□	□	□	□	□	□
36 ALL HUESCA and Province	■	■	□	□	□	□	□	□	□	□	□
37 ALL JAEN and Province	■	■	■	□	□	□	□	□	□	□	□
38 ALL ALMERIA and Province	■	■	■	■	□	□	□	□	□	□	□
39 ALL CASTELLON and the Costa del Azahar	■	■	■	■	□	□	□	□	□	□	□
40 ALL CUENCA and Province	■	■	■	■	□	□	□	□	□	□	□
41 ALL LEON and Province	■	■	■	■	□	□	□	□	□	□	□
42 ALL PONTEVEDRA, VIGO and the Rías Bajas	■	■	■	■	□	□	□	□	□	□	□
43 ALL RONDA	■	■	■	■	□	□	□	□	□	□	□
44 ALL SORIA	■	□	□	□	□	□	□	□	□	□	□

The printing of this book was completed
in the workshops of FISA - Industrias
Gráficas, Palaudarias, 26 - Barcelona
(Spain)